Mars

By Gregory Vogt

A Harcourt Company

www.steck-vaughn.com

Copyright © 2001, Steck-Vaughn Company

ISBN 0-7398-3343-X

All rights reserved. No part of this book may be reproduced or utilized in any form or by any means, electronic or mechanical, including photocopying, recording, or by any information storage and retrieval system, without permission in writing from the publisher. Inquiries should be addressed to copyright permissions, Steck-Vaughn Company, P.O. Box 26015, Austin, TX 78755.

Printed and bound in the United States of America
1 2 3 4 5 6 7 8 9 W 04 03 02 01

Photo Acknowledgments
D. Crisp (JPL), the WFPC2 Science Team, NASA, title page, 12 (top and bottom), 27, 28, 30, 34, 40, 42, 44; NASA/USGS, 6, 14, 36, 39; NASA/JPL/Malin Space Science Systems, 16, 20 (bottom), 41; NASA/JPL, 18, 32; Phil James (Univ. Toledo), Todd Clancy (Space Science Inst., Boulder, CO), Steve Lee (Univ. Colorado), and NASA, 20 (top); P. James (Univ. Toledo), T. Clancy (Space Station Inst.), S. Lee (Univ. Colorado) and NASA, 22; European Southern Observatory, 24

Contents

Diagram of Mars 4

A Quick Look at Mars 5

Fourth Planet 7

A Closer Look 15

Exploring Mars 25

Mars Today 35

Glossary 46

Internet Sites and Addresses 47

Index 48

Diagram of Mars

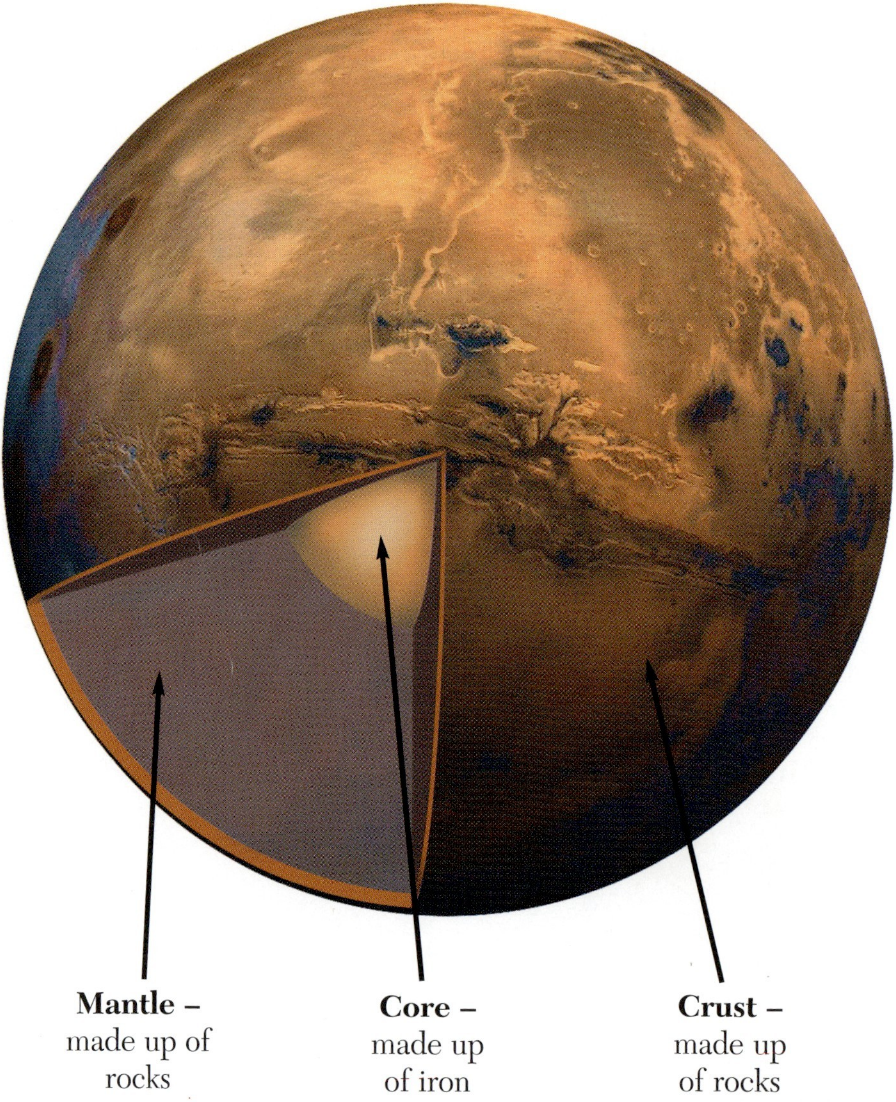

Mantle – made up of rocks

Core – made up of iron

Crust – made up of rocks

A Quick Look at Mars

Where is Mars in the solar system?
Mars is the fourth planet from the Sun. Mars is 142 million miles (228 million km) away from the Sun.

How big is Mars?
Mars is the third smallest planet in the solar system. It is 4,334 miles (6,794 km) in diameter.

What does Mars look like?
Reddish dust and soil cover Mars. The surface has volcanoes, cliffs, valleys, and flat areas called plains.

How did Mars get its name?
Mars has a reddish glow in the sky. Its red color reminded ancient people of blood and war. They named the planet after Mars, the Roman god of war.

Does Mars have any moons?
Two small moons travel around Mars. The moons are called Phobos and Deimos.

▼ **The dark areas on Mars are dark dust and hardened lava flows.**

Fourth Planet

Mars is the fourth planet from the Sun. A planet is a large object that circles a star. The Sun is a star. It is a ball of very hot gas that gives off heat and light.

The red planet is another name for Mars. From Earth, it looks like a bright orange-red star in the night sky. Light from the Sun bounces off the orange-red surface of Mars. This makes it glow like a reddish star.

Long ago, Romans and Greeks saw the red glow of Mars. The red color made them think of blood and war. They named the planet after Mars, the Roman god of war.

Mars is a part of our large solar system. The Sun and all the objects that circle around it make up our solar system.

Mars in the Solar System

Mars is one of the nine known planets that circle the Sun. The planets circle the Sun in a set order. Mars is the fourth planet from the Sun. Mercury is the first. Venus is the second. Earth is the third. All of these planets are made mostly of rock.

The Sun has the greatest gravity in the solar system because it is the most massive object. Gravity is a natural force that attracts objects to each other. Massive objects contain a great deal of mass and have greater gravity. Mass is the amount of matter an object contains. Matter is anything that has weight and takes up space. The Sun's gravity keeps all the planets and their moons circling it. Its gravity also holds smaller objects in the solar system. Without the Sun, these objects would spin away into space.

Beyond Mars is a belt of asteroids. Asteroids are large space rocks. Asteroids can be as small as cars or as large as buildings. Beyond the asteroid belt, the giant planets Jupiter, Saturn, Uranus, and Neptune circle the Sun. These planets are made mostly out of gas. Pluto is the planet farthest from the Sun. Pluto is a small planet made of ice and rock.

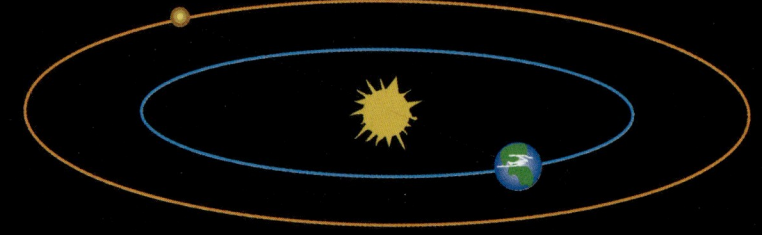

> This diagram shows the paths Mars and Earth travel as they orbit the Sun.

Orbiting the Sun

Each planet travels around the Sun in a path called an orbit. Mars is an average distance of 142 million miles (228 million km) away from the Sun. It is one and one-half times farther from the Sun than Earth is.

Planets closer to the Sun orbit faster than planets farther from the Sun. This is because the Sun's gravity is stronger when an object is closer to it. Without this speed, planets would fall into the Sun.

Mars speeds through space at 15 miles (24 km) per second. At this speed, a person could travel around the entire Earth in about 28 minutes.

Even at this speed, it takes Mars many days to travel around the Sun. A planet's year is the time it takes that planet to travel around the Sun once. It takes Mars 687 Earth days to travel around the Sun. Earth takes 365 days to circle the Sun. This means one Mars year is almost as long as about two Earth years.

Sometimes the orbit of Mars takes it close to Earth. This happens when Mars and Earth are both on the same side of the Sun. At this closest approach, they are about 35 million miles (56 million km) apart. Many astronomers study Mars during this time. Astronomers are scientists who study objects in space.

At other times, Mars and Earth are on different sides of the Sun. Then they are 235 million miles (378 million km) apart. It is harder for astronomers to study Mars when it is so far away.

▼ **Craters cover Deimos (top) and Phobos (bottom).**

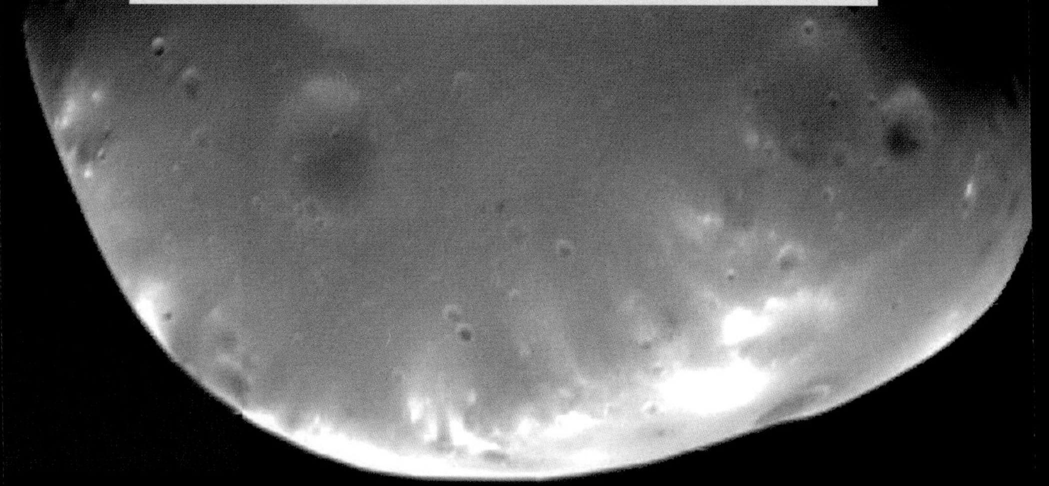

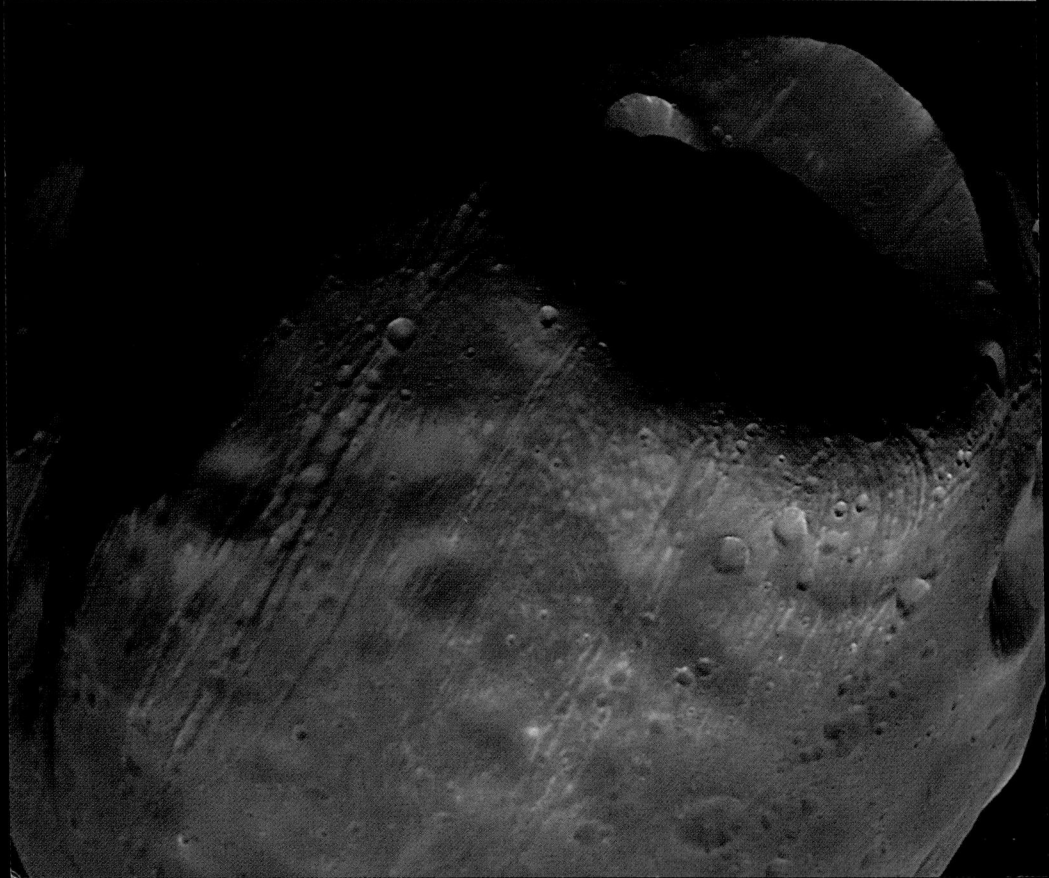

Phobos and Deimos

Two moons orbit Mars. They are called Phobos and Deimos. The moons were named after the sons of the Roman god Mars. Phobos means fear. Deimos means panic.

The moons are very small. Phobos is 17 miles (27 km) across. Deimos is 9.3 miles (15 km) across. To see the moons, people need powerful telescopes. A telescope is a tool that makes faraway objects look clearer and closer.

Phobos and Deimos are shaped like two giant potatoes. Bumps, scratches, and craters cover their surfaces. Craters are holes made when meteorites hit an object in space. A small rock floating in space is called a meteoroid. Meteoroids are called meteorites once they crash into other objects in space. Meteorites cause explosions that make bowl-shaped holes in the surface of the moons. Both moons have many craters.

Phobos orbits 3,700 miles (6,000 km) above the surface of Mars. It circles the planet once every 7.6 hours. Deimos orbits 14,562 miles (23,436 km) above Mars. It circles the planet once every 30 hours.

Astronomers believe Phobos and Deimos were once asteroids. They think the gravity of Mars pulled the asteroids into orbit around the planet.

▲ The orange and light-orange areas are smooth, dust-covered plains.

A Closer Look

Mars is the third smallest planet in the solar system. About two planets the diameter of Mars would fit into Earth. Diameter is the distance across a circle through its center. At its equator, Mars is 4,334 miles (6,794 km) in diameter. An equator is an imaginary line. It circles the middle of an object and divides it into two equal halves.

Mars has less gravity than Earth does. Gravity partly determines a person's weight. A 100-pound (46-kg) person on Earth would weigh only 38 pounds (17 kg) on Mars. Mars has about one-third the mass of Earth.

Mars has some of the largest natural features in the solar system. It has huge canyons. These are deep valleys with steep sides. It also has large volcanoes. In the past, ash, gas, and melted rock called lava blew out of openings in the tops of these mountains.

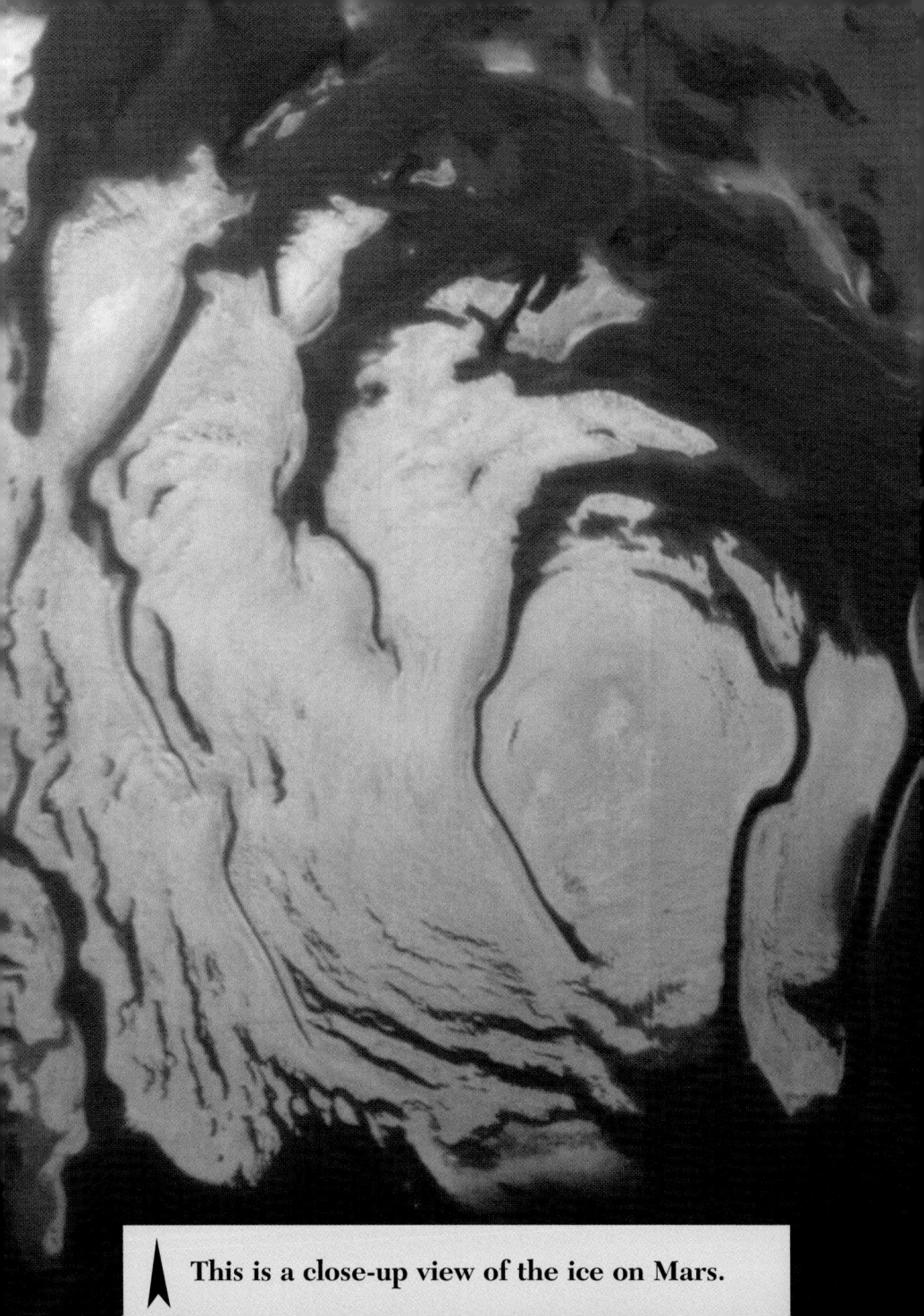

▲ This is a close-up view of the ice on Mars.

On the Surface

In the 1970s, spacecraft took the first pictures of the surface of Mars. The pictures showed scientists what Mars looked like.

The sky on Mars looks pink. Orange-red sand and dust cover the planet. The sand and dust are red because they contain the chemical iron oxide. Iron oxide is also called rust. Many large and small orange-red rocks also cover the surface of Mars. Mars has large deserts and flat areas called plains.

Pictures taken from space show many dark areas on Mars. These dark areas are large craters, mountains, cliffs, canyons, and volcanoes.

Old, dry riverbeds line the surface of Mars. Scientists believe that long ago liquid water flowed on Mars. Astronomers do not know what happened to all the water. Scientists think more water might be frozen beneath the surface of Mars.

Mars does have ice. Frozen carbon-dioxide gas forms one kind of ice on Mars. It is called dry ice because it never melts and turns into liquid. Carbon dioxide is either a gas or a solid ice. Frozen water makes up the second kind of ice. Large areas of ice called ice caps surround the North and South Poles on Mars. The northern polar ice cap is mostly water ice. The southern polar ice cap is mostly dry ice.

Thin Atmosphere

Mars does not have any liquids on its surface because they would boil away. It is not heat that would make the water boil. Mars only reaches about 70° Fahrenheit (21° C). This amount of heat is not enough to boil water even on Earth.

The atmosphere on Mars would make any water boil. An atmosphere is a layer of gases that surrounds a planet. Mars has a very thin atmosphere. It is much thinner than Earth's atmosphere. Water quickly boils without the weight of a thick atmosphere pressing down. In fact, most liquids would quickly boil. Even a person's blood would boil on Mars.

The atmosphere of Mars is mostly carbon-dioxide gas. People and animals breathe out carbon-dioxide gas. They breathe in oxygen. Mars has very little oxygen. Without more oxygen, people could not live on Mars. They could not live by breathing in carbon dioxide.

Today, most of Mars is covered with dry dust and rocks.

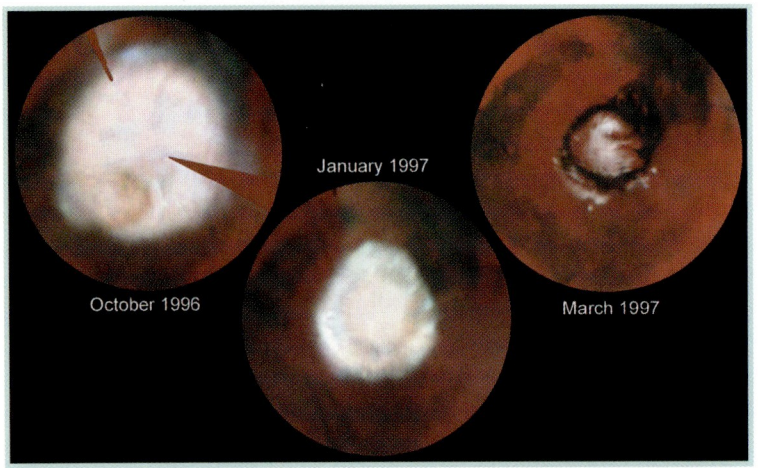

This series of photographs shows how much ice melts as it grows warmer on Mars (above). The polar ice cap (below) changes depending on the season.

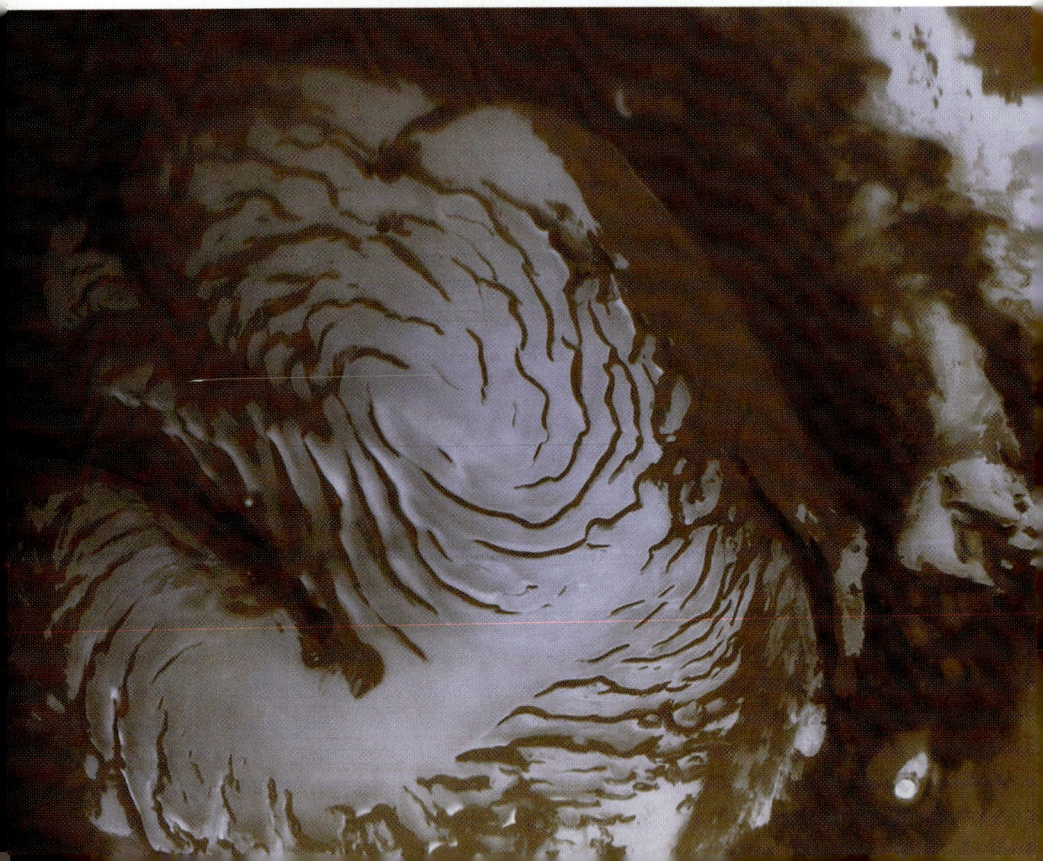

Seasons

Mars spins like all planets do. A planet's spin is called its rotation. The amount of time it takes a planet to rotate once is that planet's day. It takes Mars 24 hours and 37 minutes to make one complete rotation. This means that a day on Mars is 37 minutes longer than a day on Earth.

Some planets have seasons because they slowly tilt toward or away from the Sun as they orbit. Mars has seasons too. For part of the year, Mars's North Pole tilts toward the Sun. The North Pole receives more sunlight and becomes warmer. It is then summer in the northern half of Mars. At the same time, the South Pole tilts away from the Sun. It receives less sunlight and becomes colder. It is then winter in the southern half.

Later in the year, the North Pole points away from the Sun. The South Pole tilts toward the Sun. It is then winter in the north and summer in the south.

Mars's polar ice caps change depending on the season. Polar ice caps grow larger during winter. They shrink during summer.

▲ Scientists took this series of pictures to show a huge dust storm blowing across Mars. The storm looks like a thin, white cloud.

Weather

Mars has different kinds of weather. Sometimes light winds blow on Mars. On other days, strong winds blow across the planet. Strong winds stir up dust from the surface. The storms can last for days or months. At times, the atmosphere becomes full of dust. Astronomers cannot see the surface of Mars when this happens.

The average temperature on Mars is about –70° Fahrenheit (–57° C). A warm day on Mars is around 70° Fahrenheit (21° C). A cold day on Mars is much colder than the coldest days on Earth. In winter, the temperature at Mars's poles can drop to –195° Fahrenheit (–126° C).

Temperatures during winter on Mars are cold enough to freeze carbon dioxide in the atmosphere. The dry ice falls to the surface of Mars like snow. It covers parts of the polar areas with a thin, white coating of ice.

Some features on Mars are named after famous astronomers. This is a picture of the Schiaparelli Hemisphere. It is named after Giovanni Schiaparelli.

Exploring Mars

Many astronomers use telescopes to study the surface of Mars. But sometimes astronomers make mistakes about what they think they see.

In 1877, Giovanni Schiaparelli used a telescope to study Mars. Schiaparelli thought he saw lines crisscrossing the surface of Mars. He thought the lines looked like canals. He told other astronomers about what he saw. Not all astronomers believed this. But some said they saw the canals, too.

Many people thought the canals proved that there was life on Mars. They thought life forms called Martians must have dug the canals to move water across the dry planet.

Early Missions to Mars

At the very closest point in its orbit, Mars is still 35 million miles (56 million km) away from Earth. The surface of Mars looks fuzzy even through very powerful telescopes. Scientists must send spacecraft to Mars to see what Mars really looks like. The spacecraft send pictures of Mars back to scientists on Earth.

Scientists have sent more than 30 spacecraft to Mars. About half of the spacecraft never reached the planet. They either crashed, missed the planet, or stopped working before they reached Mars.

Mars 1 was the first spacecraft scientists tried to send to Mars. On November 1, 1962, *Mars 1* took off from the Soviet Union. Scientists lost radio contact with the spacecraft. The mission failed.

In 1964, scientists in the United States tried to send a spacecraft to Mars. *Mariner 3* had problems, too. Its protective covering did not fall off when it left Earth's gravity. Because of this, it could not use its solar panels for energy. It ran out of power when its batteries died. It failed to reach Mars.

On November 28, 1964, U.S. scientists launched the *Mariner 4* spacecraft. Its mission was a success. It flew past Mars on July 15, 1965. As it flew by Mars, it snapped 22 close-up pictures of the surface

▲ **This black-and-white picture shows some of the sand dunes on Mars.**

of Mars. There were no Martian-made canals. There were dry river channels and craters.

Mariner 5 failed to reach Mars. But in 1969, both Mariner 6 and Mariner 7 reached Mars. Mariner 6 took 75 pictures of the surface. Mariner 7 took 126 pictures of Mars. Mariner 8 failed to reach Mars. Because of these Mariner missions, astronomers began to see what the surface of Mars looked like.

Mariner 9 took several hundred pictures of Mars.

Mariner 9

The United States sent *Mariner 9* into the orbit of Mars in 1971. When it began orbiting, a big dust storm covered the surface of Mars. At first, *Mariner 9* could only take pictures of the dust clouds. Over time, the dust storm stopped.

The spacecraft began taking more pictures as soon as the dust cleared. *Mariner 9* discovered many new features on Mars. It took pictures of deep valleys and giant volcanoes. It found channels on Mars that looked like streams or river valleys. *Mariner 9* took pictures of marks left on the surface by strong windstorms.

Mariner 9 took hundreds of pictures. The pictures helped astronomers learn what the surface of Mars looks like. They also studied the *Mariner 9* pictures to find places to land future spacecraft. They wanted to be ready for new missions to the red planet.

▶ This picture from *Viking* shows the rocks and the orange-pink sky of Mars.

The Viking Missions

The United States launched two spacecraft to Mars in 1975. These spacecraft were *Viking 1* and *Viking 2*. Each *Viking* spacecraft had two parts. The first part was a large spacecraft built to orbit Mars. The second part was a lander. The lander was built to drop down from the orbiting spacecraft and land on the surface of Mars. The Viking missions were the first to place landers on Mars.

The *Viking* spacecraft began to orbit Mars in 1976. They took pictures of Mars and sent them to Earth. Scientists looked at the pictures and found places for the landers to touch down. Mission controllers released the landers one month after the spacecraft began to orbit. Mission controllers operate spacecraft from Earth.

The landers fell toward Mars. Parachutes slowed them down. This umbrella-shaped fabric helped them land gently on the surface.

Each *Viking* lander had two cameras that took pictures and sent them back to Earth. The landers had instruments to check the weather and the soil on Mars. They had machines to measure any movement, such as earthquakes, of the surface of Mars.

Each lander also had a robotic arm. Mission controllers sent commands from Earth to the lander. The lander did what the controllers instructed. It used the arm to scoop up Martian soil.

The *Viking* landers checked the soil for living things. Scientists disagree about the results of the experiments. Some think there are signs of life, but other scientists disagree. Scientists want to do more tests and keep looking for life on Mars.

▼ *Sojourner* studied rocks and soil samples.

Pathfinder and *Sojourner*

In 1996, the United States sent *Pathfinder* into space. *Pathfinder* carried a rover called *Sojourner*. The rover was a small robot car. Scientists sent instructions to *Sojourner* from Earth.

Pathfinder landed on Mars on July 4, 1997. Huge airbags inflated and surrounded the spacecraft when it landed. *Pathfinder* bounced twice when it hit the surface of Mars. The airbags protected the spacecraft during this bumpy landing.

After it stopped moving, mission controllers let the air out of the bags. *Pathfinder*'s instruments began measuring the weather. Its cameras sent pictures back to Earth.

Mission controllers opened *Pathfinder's* petal-like doors. A ramp unrolled. Then they steered the rover *Sojourner* forward onto the planet's surface. Mission controllers moved the car around rocks and over the surface of Mars.

Sojourner had spiked wheels, so it could travel across the soil on Mars. It carried instruments to study rocks. The instruments measured what the rocks were made of.

Sojourner and *Pathfinder* worked for 90 days until they ran out of power. Scientists are still studying the information they gathered.

▲ **This picture shows what Valles Marineris looks like from space.**

Mars Today

Pictures sent to Earth from spacecraft have taught scientists a lot about Mars. Today, we know more about the amazing features that make up the surface of the red planet.

Valles Marineris is a huge canyon cut into the surface of Mars. Parts of the canyon are more than 125 miles (201 km) wide. Some parts of it are 5 miles (8 km) deep. It is about 2,500 miles (4,022 km) long. It stretches about one-fifth of the way around the planet. This makes the canyon longer than the width of the United States.

A crack in the surface of Mars started the giant Martian canyon. Over time, wind, landslides, and water widened and deepened the canyon.

 Olympus Mons is a giant volcano like the Mauna Loa volcano in Hawaii.

Giant Volcanoes

All of the mountains on Mars are volcanoes. Volcanoes form when hot lava pours out of cracks in a planet's surface. Lava cools and hardens when it pours out onto the surface. Then more lava pours out and piles up. Over time, very large mountains form.

The volcanoes on Mars are much larger than those on Earth. Volcanoes on Earth do not grow as tall as Mars's volcanoes because Earth's crust is made up of plates of slowly moving rock. Over many years, Earth's plates move and push volcanoes away from the hot lava cracks. The volcanoes stop growing. New volcanoes form over the lava cracks.

Many years ago, the surface of Mars might have been made of moving plates. But scientists think that plates on Mars are not moving anymore. The rock on Mars does not move. So volcanoes were able to grow for a very long time and become giants. The Martian volcanoes only stopped growing when there was no more lava. Scientists have not found any active volcanoes on Mars yet.

Olympus Mons is a giant volcano that rises 16 miles (25 km) above the surface of Mars. Its base is about 374 miles (550 km) wide. The base covers as much area as the state of Missouri. Olympus Mons is the largest volcano in the solar system. It is about three times as tall as the 5.5-mile (9-km) high Mount Everest. Mount Everest is the tallest mountain on Earth.

Channels

Mariner 9 discovered channels on Mars. These channels on Mars are too small to be seen with telescopes from Earth.

Astronomers believe ancient rivers carved the channels. Water that flowed across the surface carried rock and sand away. Today, twisting dry channels are all that is left of the rivers.

Scientists think the water that made the channels came from beneath the surface of Mars. Ice beneath the surface may have melted and released the water. Heat from the volcanoes may have melted the ice. Giant meteorites striking Mars might have also released water. Astronomers think some of the water boiled away into space. Some of it has frozen in the soil at the North and South Poles. Scientists think more water may be beneath the planet's surface.

In June 2000, *Mars Global Surveyor* took new, close-up pictures of Mars. Some scientists believe these pictures prove that there may be some liquid water on Mars today or in the recent past. The pictures showed features that look like gullies. A gully is a long, narrow ditch. Scientists think moving water formed the gullies on Mars. They believe water from beneath Mars's surface flooded the land. They do not know what caused the flooding.

▲ This 373-mile (600-km) long river channel drained into a large crater when water flowed through it.

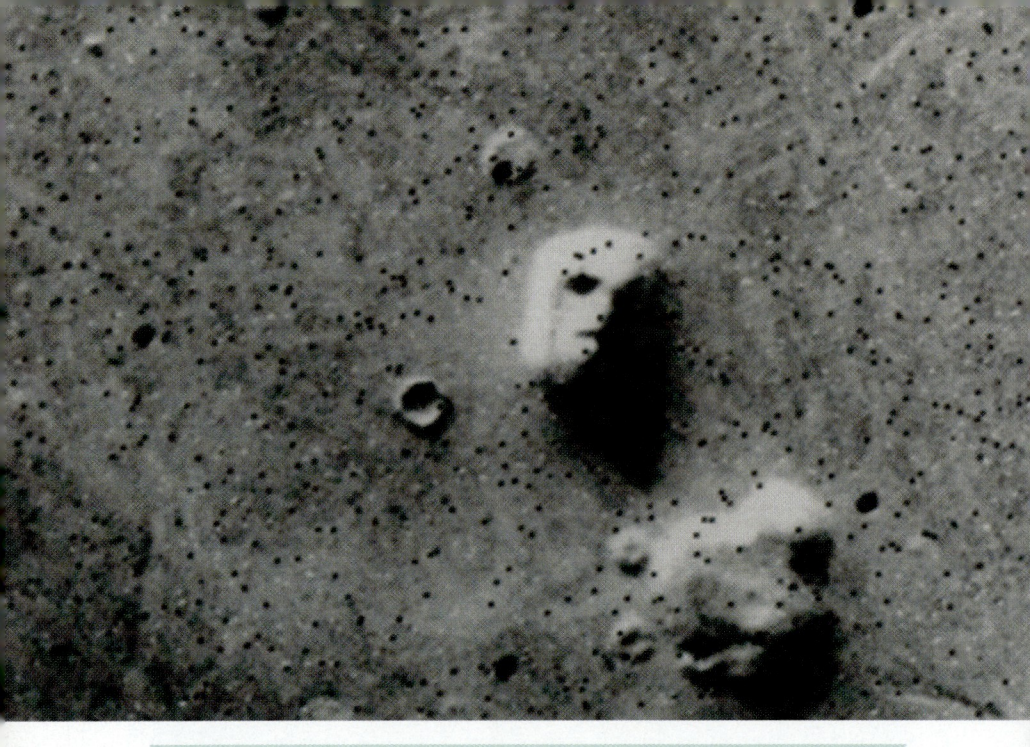

▲ In 1976, *Viking* took a picture of a 1-mile (1.6-km) long rock formation that looked like a face.

Face on Mars

The *Viking* spacecraft that circled Mars in the 1970s took many pictures. One of the pictures showed what looked like a large face on the surface of Mars. The picture was rough and fuzzy. But it seemed to show a giant face staring into space.

Scientists studied the picture. They said the face was a natural rock formation. Others believed the face was carved into the rock by Martians. They thought Martians made the face just like people on Earth have carved rocks into shapes.

▲ **This picture of the same rock formation was taken with a powerful camera in 1997.**

The *Mars Global Surveyor* began orbiting Mars in 1997. It used new, high-powered cameras to take pictures of the face.

The face was really a hill. Shadows of rocks on the hill made it look like a face. Natural forces have also made many rocks on Earth look like faces or animals. Wind, water, ice, and snow have carved these rocks into strange shapes. From space, the rocks might look like people or animals.

▲ Scientists are still looking for life in the rocks and soil on Mars.

Life on Mars

Many people have made up stories about Martians. There are many movies and books about Martians attacking Earth. Some TV shows are about Martians living on Earth.

No one knows if there is life on Mars. Scientists do not know what living things on Mars would look like. The *Viking* spacecraft have already looked for life on Mars. They found no evidence of life.

The surface of Mars is not a good place for living things to grow. Living things on Earth need certain things to survive. People and animals need water to drink and oxygen to breathe. Mars gets very cold. All the water on the planet is frozen. Mars has very little oxygen in its atmosphere.

Still, it is possible that there may be life on Mars. Life can be found in strange places on Earth. Some plants live in snow. Other plants live in the boiling water at Yellowstone National Park. Still other life is found inside of rocks.

Scientists want to find out if Mars has any living things. Much life on Earth is underground. If there is liquid water underground on Mars, there may be living things underneath Mar's surface. Scientists plan to keep searching for life on Mars.

▲ Scientists are studying this meteorite from Mars. They took this picture with a ruler to show how big the rock is.

The Mars Rock

Sometimes large meteorites strike Mars. This causes explosions. The explosions blast some rock from Mars into space. Scientists believe that some of this rock has fallen to Earth.

In 1984, a scientist named Roberta Score found a rock in Antarctica. She gave the rock to the space program in the United States.

In 1996, scientists began studying the rock. They discovered the rock was like rocks from Mars. They found tiny specks inside the rock. Some scientists think these specks might be fossils. A fossil is the remains of a living thing from another time period. Not all scientists agree that the specks are fossils from Mars. More study will be needed to be sure what they are.

Scientists will keep trying to find out about life on Mars. Future astronauts may travel to Mars. They will try to find fossils in rocks. They will also explore the ice and ancient river channels on Mars. They will drill to try and reach underground water. Maybe life exists in the ice or in the soil beneath the channels.

Mars is the planet that is most similar to Earth. Some scientists believe people could live on Mars someday. They are trying to figure out ways for people to explore and live safely on Mars.

Glossary

asteroid (ASS-tuh-roid)—a large space rock orbiting the Sun

astronomer (uh-STRON-uh-mer)—a scientist who studies objects in space

atmosphere (AT-muhss-fihr)—a layer of gases that surrounds a planet

crater (KRAY-tur)—bowl-shaped hole left when a meteorite strikes an object in space

lander (LAN-dur)—spacecraft that lands on another planet

Martian (MAR-shuhn)—fictional life forms from Mars

meteorite (MEE-tee-ur-rite)—a rock that crashes into the surface of an object in space

orbit (OR-bit)—the path an object travels in around another object in space

rotation (roh-TAY-shuhn)—the spinning of an object in space

solar system (SOH-lur SISS-tuhm)—the Sun and all the objects that orbit around it

spacecraft (SPAYSS-craft)—machine that travels through space

telescope (TEL-uh-skope)—a tool that makes faraway objects appear clearer and closer

Internet Sites and Addresses

Center for Mars Exploration
http://cmex-www.arc.nasa.gov

Mars Pathfinder
http://mpfwww.jpl.nasa.gov/MPF/index.html

The Mars Society
http://www.marssociety.org

Star Child: A Learning Center for Young Astronomers
http://starchild.gsfc.nasa.gov/docs/StarChild

NASA Headquarters
Washington, DC 20546-0001

The Mars Society
P.O. Box 272
Indian Hills, CO 80454

Index

asteroid, 8, 13
atmosphere, 19, 43

canal, 25, 26
canyon, 15, 17, 35
crater, 13, 17, 26

Deimos, 13

equator, 15

gravity, 8, 11, 13, 15
Greeks, 7

ice cap, 17, 21

Mercury, 8
meteor, 13
meteorite, 13, 38, 45

Olympus Mons, 37
orbit, 10, 11, 26, 30

Pathfinder, 33
Phobos, 13

red planet, 7, 35
Romans, 7
rotation, 21

Saturn, 8
Schiaparelli, Giovanni, 25
seasons, 21
Sojourner, 33
solar system, 7, 8, 15
star, 7
Sun, 7, 8, 10, 11, 21

telescope, 13, 25, 26

Valles Marineris, 35
Viking, 30-31, 40, 43
volcano, 15, 17, 29, 36-37, 38